I WRITE BECAUSE NO ONE LISTENS

ALI ASHRAF

Contents

Acknowledgements

This is Md Ali Ashraf, And ultimately i have completed this book with lots of enjoyment and enthusiasm.The best thing about this book is whatever i have written in this is purely from my bottom of my heart.What i have experienced in my life,whatever i have gone through ups and down in my life,what i have learnt from my life till now,all my experienced is shared in just a bundle of pages.I am not a professional writer,but i have tried my utmost level to share valuable and informative life lessons to the people who have read this.I hope you have enjoyed a lot and thanks to myself and thanks to my publication who have supported me for publishing this book.And most importantly thanks to my readers,immense love for you all that you have taken out your precious time and read this book.I hope you'll enjoy while reading this.Hope,i will come again with another great content later.Thanks to all,love you all,be safe and enjoy your life.

ONE

LOVE IS CONFUSING

Heyyyy..!!! A dynamic and Warm Welcome To All Of You To This Majestic Book. Lets First Smile Just now To Make Yourself happy before Commencing This Wonderful Story..Hope you All Are Under The Shelter Of Protection and Don't Despair untill The Humanity Prevails. The Journey from Age 15 to 25 is full of Energetic,Depression,True Love To A Wrong Person,,Family Issues And Some Heart Wrenching Feelings Which is always Inside Our Heart But never Came Out..Between These years We Are Most Terrified With A Word "Fear".The Fear Of Losing Your Love,Fear Of Failing In Exams,Fear Of Freak Society,Fear Of Passing years and You Are Same as You were used to be Before 2 years Ago ,Fear Of Not Achieving The Goal..!!!

But you know what In between All these Something Which Always keeps Going is "Ray Of Hope"..I don't know I will Conquer The Match or Not but I have a Hope That I Can.I don't Know I can become a Actor Or Not but deep inside my heart Says I have A hope That I Can.I Even

Haven't Filled Even 5 Pages Properly but I have A Hope That I will pass in Exam And Move To Next Stage Of My Life As I Always Do.I Have Lost My Everything And My Family Perception For me is Nothing As I Am Worthless To See Grin On their Face, I Am a Monochrome Person With Nothing Fascinating And No One Even Give a Shitt to me And I Am Totally Depressed With My Life. But QuesTion is Why I am Still Alive?That's The Way Life Continues..A Hope That Something Will Come to My life and Everything Will Change one day. "HOPE" Is The Most Powerful Weapon In The Brain

When My Hormones Are Stimulating And My WhoLe body structure is Changing, My Mind Is Confronting Each and Every Situation Of My Life, I am Learning From weird Society What Bad Impact And Repercussion Had been On Me Perhaps I am Going Far Away From My Shenanigans(Childish Behaviour) And There was a Time When No Reason To Enjoy The WhoLe day And Coming Back Home and Again Enjoying With Different Stuffs, We Didn't Ever Bother What The Consequences Will Be of Any Actions..We Were in that Level of Happiness. If Today We Even reimagine of Those Moments Literally We can't Man..The Only Stuff We were Frightened About Is Parents Teacher Meeting.I know You Are Smiling Right Now .Well Thats The Truth And Veracity Of UnderAge..!!!

But What Happen Now? I am losing my liberty, I am Going Away From my Authentic Happiness As I used to be before,I am Losing My Childhood School Morning,Canteen,Evening Enjoyment, Going To Grandpaa Home And Fear That Ending of Summer Vacation is soon, Fear Of Father If Something Wrong I will Commit He Will Make My Smooth Cheeks And bum Red, Fear Of Mother and her Intimidation that If I will Not Come To Home On

Time She Has A Long Broom For My Invitation To Home..Man Literally My Eyes Are Weeping Now Not for Moments That Had Gone but I am Feeling Heart Wrenching More that those Moments Will Never Ever Come Back.I said Never..!!! Now Everything Is Volatile,We really Don't Know When We All Grew Up.Each and Everything Circumstancing Around us Is Objectionable To Us That Why Is it Happening To Me?

The Questions starts Arising in Our Most Powerful Weapon Brain.Is I Am The Worst? Why My destiny Is Not Like Others? Why Am I Black? Why I am so Pudgy? We are So much Obsessed That Sometimes We Ask To ourself Why My Jawline is Not Like A Particular Person. But Wait What? Do You Ever conceive that why These Questions Never arises in Childhood? Because We Have A Sublime Humor and Positive Perception in Teenager That Makes Us Happiness And Ravingly Matters to me Regardless Of The Feelings Complexity..If Going Out in a Rainy Season and Playing Football In a Mud Soil Makes me Happy..Then Bring It On..If Making Fun Of Teachers Makes me Blissful I will never Going To say No becuase My Happiness Matters To Me The Most!!!

But now Whole Concept Has Changed.We are Addicted To Feelings,Priorities,,Narcissism and Obsessions. If Anyone Is Sophisticated and Superior Then You The Mind Will Prevalently Ask Why I am Not Good as Him? Why I am Not getting Priorities And Prestige As They? Why Someone Have More feeling For Particular Individual and Not For Me? And Believe me Feelings is The Most Constructive And Destructive ParT of Human Nature.Thats the Distinctive Between Childhood And Now Where We Are..All these Aspiration and Wishes Keeps Our Within Happiness And Kind Hearted Soul Away From Us...!!

The Most Veracity Of This Youth is Falling In Love..No I am not talking About Parents Or Society Love..The love Which May Makes you Stronger or May Makes You HighLy Vulnerable..A Moment will Come in Your life when You Will Fall For Him/Her.Its Not Something you are committing Crime To do so,its a human Nature,It is ok To Love Someone,you and I Should accept That.Saying that Loving anyone is a Crime and Comes Under Bad Elements is Totally Silly And Preposterous Folk.You can Fall for which You Have a Separate Emotion For That Special.Or Perhaps You will Have Infatuation for Someone.I am not here to tell you that love is blind or love is fake..Fake Love Is Totally Hypothetical to Those Who Loves Truely..And True Love Is Hypothetical for Those whose HearT has Been Thrown Into The Garbage by That Person which He has Faith At Once.It is All About Priorities and Interest...!!!

You will fall for Someone..Now The Countdown Starts.Everything Starts Changing within You,Your Way Of Talking,Your Way Of Considering Yourself,Your way Of Thinking Just Because You Will Feel Special And Out Of Billions people He/She Loves me Unconditionally That What makes You Feel Proud Within Yourself.Feeling Special And Confidence inside yourself is the biggest reason To be Happy.You will Love Your Guest Of Your Life From your Pure Heart As first Love is Unconditional and From The Inner Soul.It is True That Loves Teaches You More Then You Have Learnt In in School.Loving The Right Person Will Make your life More Easier,Happier, And Most Important You Will Feel Special For Range Of Time..!!!

But What If you are broken..Ahh Its Devastating,Your heart Will Shattered.Now from here the reality Begins..Now You will Grasp The weird Society and People better then You used to Consider them before.You Will feel The

Importance of Yourself now When You Had given your 100% to someone else And In Return You Get To Realise The Reality of this Fake World..U will Know The Value of Self Respect and The Quality in You Which you Never Saw within you Because You were busy in Some Shitty Love.Yes If True Love Can change a person then Fake Love can can Change A Person Unexpectedly And More Stronger and Harder..!!!.

But You Know what It is ok To fall In Love Once in Life..If You Will Not Go Inside the Swimming Pool how will you learn the Swimming? You just cant read book how to swim and you will learn to swim.No Life doesn't Go in that way.In the same Way Falling In Love and Knowing the Priorities and Precedence Is What Makes You Practical..Love can take you Where you would have never expected or Prognosticated. Choosing The Nobility And Wisest Person And Experiencing The Wrong Person in Your life will make You Stronger and Restorative.Ahh Love Has So Many Variation.Really Love is Unpredictable..I Repeat Love is Unpredictable...!!!

TWO

JEALOUSY

The Love Word Is Very Symmetrical To "Jealousy".Ahh The Word Which No one Talk Often and Frequently,Everyone Can Just feel Inside.Jealousy of Having The Mindset That Someone is Superior than you.Jealousy Makes You feel Inferior,If someone has That Innate quality That is Exceptional and Quarreling on This Is Goofy and Moron Act.But if Anyone has Earned by his perseverance,Its His/ Her choice And Its their Hard Work..Accept the Reality That Jealousy Is The Most Hidden Word inside Your Mind And Heart And It Will be Always In Your Subconscious Mind.The Conscious Mind Will Operate Your Jealousy Inside The Subconscious Mind..!!

Basically my Question is Having Jealousy of Envy and Desire Of Something Is ok but Keeping That Jealousy Constantly Circulating In Your brain and Life is Always Your Mistake and Maybe It Will have The Worst Impact on you.You have a Choice,You have an Opportunity,You have The Liberty of doing What is Best For You Then Why can't you Change yourself to get rid of That Jealousy? Having Jealousy For Something Will Always Keep You Away From Who You are Actually And Maybe Your Asset Can Be in a

Crypto State ..Jealousy Can Be Most Destructive For Your Entire Body..!!!

I Am not Talking About The Innate Quality or Characteristic of a Person.This is Precisionly Exceptional So The best way to Confront this Type of Jealousy is to Accept the fact And Confess your Soul That ok God Must Be Having Some Plan That's Why They are Different And I am Different from them.But You will Be Always Yourself.Tell Yourself I am The Best in My Own Way And No One is like Me.Really you are Special..You are the Best.Believe me You have so much Qualities Inside you but you never let it come because you were busy Comparing with Others.Take Out your best Version Of yourself.Even Your Own DNA can't resemble to anyone in this whole Planet..So How can You think You are not like others..You are You,You are Unique, You are special and Distinctive..!!!

You Consider Yourself Everywhere on The Judgment Of Your Qualities..You Know Every Negative And Positive Aspects Inside You..Some Good and Cheesy Qualities inside you is Just Yours and only you knows inside your heart,Mind and Every part of your Body.Why you are Jealous Of Someone?Because You keep Striving and Endeavoring To Defeat someone but the Fact is you are not doing anything to Improve Yourself.No one has come here With Knowledge and Wisdom from her mother Womb.You have to Work hard with Full determination and Perseverance To Dominate or Defeat Anyone To overcome the Most Weird Word Jealousy..!!

Why you are Jealous to Someone.Why you are not Improving and Getting Mentally and Physically Developed?Because You don't Want To Do Tough and Become Tough..Toughness is Pertinent to Laziness,No Life Wants Something Else.Work harder and harder until the

Success Prevails And You Will feel One day Within Inside That There is No such Word Inside Me Jealousy.I am Not Imparting That Desire of Being Jealous Will Scrap Away at A Particular Point but You will be different,You will improve,You will be far better from Many.There is No Any Second Option.Persistence,Hardship and Consistent is The Key To Overcome Jealousy. Intelligence has No connection with Jealousy. Intelligence is maybe innate or I can firmly say you that Perseverance,Consistency,And Hardship Can Beat the Intelligencer..!!

Maybe Someone is More Handsome/Beautiful then you.Its ok There is No need to Feel Inferior in this because Beauty Attracts For A Particular Time Period Only,But the Inner Beauty will attract The Soul Inside You..Believe Me The person With a charming face and A Black Heart Will Never Be In Someone Heart Always..It Will Only Be for A range of time but the Person with Real Beauty and Pure soul Will Attract Each and Every Part of Human Soul and That Individual Will Be Always In Your Heart and Whenever You will Encounter Them A Charming Smile Will be Always on your Face..Learn To Be Attractive in a Simple way..That is The Purest Beauty..!!!

Don't Be Worried Of Being Jealous.A Jealousy Will Make You More Jealous,You will feel Suffocation from inside,A fake Smile Will be Always on your Face Whenever You will Encounter with The Once you are Jealous of.So Dont be fake,fake people never rise in Life and they will never feel Peace From inside.You are far better from those who are still Striving To Reach Your Level..Work On The Stuffs Despite been Overthinking About Them.Working and Keeping Yourself Busy In A Positive way will Keep All The Negative Thoughts Away from You.Thank To Yourself Where you are right now but Don't Be Stagnant,Learn

Something,Improve Yourself,Constantly Grow You Mind to Defeat the Jealousness....!!

Don't Be Jealous If Someone Is More Wealthy And Lives Their Life Ravishly..Remember Bill Gates Once Said If You Are Born Poor Its Not Your Mistake But If You Will Die Poor Its Your Mistake.Working and Struggling For Years And Years And Then Be at A position Where you Wanted to be Always Is The Best Achievement and Success In Life.Every Rich People is Not Flourished With Knowledge And Wisdom, they can't Achieve everything In Life With The Money.Don't always Say I am Poor and Consider them are As Supermacy.No Don't say But In Spite of that,Say No Problem Now I am Under My desires but I will do it one day,I will do it for Myself,My Parents and Freaky Society.Remember Your Life will be at The Top If You Follow Your Honesty and Integrity..!!!

Think big With doing Small Steps,Never Be A Narrow Minded Person,Never.If you are lacking Something in your Life,Its okk be positive,Indoctrinate your Mind With A Positive and Intellectual Thoughts.Remember One Thing Starting with a Positive Small Steps will be the Biggest Reason To Your Success.Don't Despair Yourself Because Just you were born poor,No this is Goofy and Preposterous Thinking.Everyone has The Equal Brain When they are born and the Only Distinctive is Some Utilize in a Best way So They Give their outcome Best.Don't Be Jealous.."You are the Best Poor In The World".Work Hard until You Conquer..!!

Having Jealousy Is Totally ok And If You Have Jealousy Then It Means Your Mind Is Continuously Operating a Question and Somewhere in Your Heart It Keeps Aching Why A Particular individual Or Why Any Specific Folk is Considered To Be Superior.You will Start Questioning

Yourself.Why I am not like that?Why I am So Moron? Why I Dont have Clothes Like Him?Why Is His Family So Orthodox and Liberal? No Man All these Question have a Single Answer..Do Your Best and Do What Needs to be the Best.Everyone in Life is At a Particular Point and In A Line of Limitation.But Instill that Everything has a Limit And There is No Obligation To Cross that Limit for a Positive Mindset..!!!

The People Around Your Circumstance Will Make The biggest Impact on your Life.Yes Your Surrounding Matters To you a Lot,You may not be aware of your Thoughts because Your Way of Behaving,Grasping,Observing The Stuffs and Surroundings are in Your Subconscious Mind,Your Mind Is Circulated By your Company,Knowingly or Unknowingly,Your each and Every Situation of your action and reaction will be Saved in your mind,And that's the way you react to the society,Whats the outcome of your Mind is what you take inside your Mind.Your Mind is very susceptible to the Pleasure Stuffs Regardless of of the Consequences..!!

You Work according To Your Mind But Your Mind Dont Work According To You.There is No Conciliation And Friendship between You and Your Mind until and unless you will not learn how to control your Mind.Keeping the Mind in your control will Keep Your Every Thought and Perception in a stable way.Learn to control Your Mind Till the extent you can.I told You Its the Biggest and Most Toxic Weapon In Your Body,Even Your Physical Is Operated by your Mentality.There is a Raving Possibility that if Your Mentality Is not healthy,Your Physically cant be Attractive.If Your Mind Is Not in Your Control You cant even Speculate Where You Life can Take You.Every perspective of yours will instill in your mind,so choose what is always soothing and Indispensable for you..!!

Virtually All these Depends on your Surrounding and Company.So Choose the Wisest And Virtue Company Around you.A Malicious And Vicious Person will Only Makes Your Mind With Full of Negativity and Garbage,You will Feel Happy For a Particular period of time but your mind is drowning into The Corrupt River.It will Never Be saturated,Feed And Feed with kindness and Generosity until you breath,Do you ever Heard Somewhere that Negative Person Has Problem of Every Solution and this is Authentic, be Honest and Scrupulous to yourself,Being Mendacious and lying to Yourself will harm you only,Keep that in Mind.Detour Your Wrong Path and Be With Those Who is Trustful and Reliable,You Will come out as a Good Person Impulsively From the Good Surrounding and Circumstance..!!

I told you that Your Total Power is In Your Subconscious Mind Which You will never perceive but It Will Continuously Regulate Your Mind.Don't be overly happy if something happens in your favor,Person doesn't give the Response from the brain when they are overjoyed,its ok to be euphoric but don't reveal everything in over happiness,We often Reveal Stuffs which should be not revealed so be vigilant,not everyone will enjoy your happiness.Always share your happiness and Predicament to whom you Are Reliable,they will keep your trust Always.Talk Good,Listen Good,Be with be the positivity,Surround Yourself With Lots of love and Inspiration,Every Single Steps matters in Your Life.Be An Inspiration to the Whole Society and Be proud of Yourself who You Are..!!

Learn and Then propogate Your Wisdom To Everyone Who Needs It.Propogating Wisdom and Knowledge To someone will keep you proud from inner of yourslef.Be a Humble Man,Dont be a boast person,Boast person will have the qualitity sometimes,but thier boastness will suppress thier Quality.In the Same way Your Action And Way of Responding and Giving Emphasize To The Society Matters,You have heard Every Action has its equal And Opposite Reaction.But it doesn't mean don't give Emphasize those who are not worth of you.No I don't mean to say That,Respect the humanity Regardless of thier Position,Standered or Status.Your discipline and Decency Towards the community will make you Lift up but Remember Dont Quarrell for irrelevant and irrational talks to the Stupid Peoples,they only want to attract your attention to themselves,dont waste time proving you are the best.Prove it to the Best Ones..!!

Embed in you brain that always be away From Stereotype People,They will only Keep Your Mind Away From The Prestigious and Lovable Stuffs.Stereotype people will never love you,If Someone is close to you and always topple you to the stereotypes talks which will make you uncomfortable and Miserable,cut the wire with Them.You are not born to Be a narrow minded Person or to have oppression to surround with them.Be Smart,And Be With Smartest ones.I am not talking About your Abs,Biceps or Face Smartness don't be happy too much,you are already smart because you are reading my book, Haha Jokes apart, Do smartness With Your Intelligence,Good People Around You Will Always Teach You New Things and The Things which You were not aware before.Learning And Grasping Consistently Good Stuffs will make you grow Spiritually and Mentally Both..!!

Your Perspective with Specific will describe Your Attitude,Live In Present But Always Prepare for the Future

Each And Everyday,Your Future is in your hand,this is a veracity,the way you build yourself each and every day will define your Prognostication.Insist Your Intellectuality And use in a sagacious way,always show grace to other people,grace is very expensive gift if you have it.You can't become Great In one day.Consistency Striving and Urging yourself towards your Aspiration will Make You someone Whom You always Envy.Learn to be With The Greatest People Around You,They are The one who Will teach You And Exhort you What You Implicitly Deserve..!!

Your Whole Life Depends on your own Perspective and Perception Towards the Community.You can't blame anyone else for your own fate and unsuccess,if you are unable to accomplish something,at least there is a slight possibility that you are missing something from your hardwork and determination,don't give up until you feel complacency and self satisfaction.Every great work needs a courage and time to accomplish it,if you don't have these qualities,you better work on these qualities first.You have a Thousand Reason that you can't achieve your desire and Dream but you know what man If You Really have a aspiration and desire to do or achieve something in life then you will find Atleast One solid and consummate Reason to do it.

Giving Excuses may have two reasons,Either You want to procrastinate it or you are not Interested in it.If you really have a profound Aspiration to achieve any Goal then do it Whatever It takes until Your Capability Exist.Always Praise and admire yourself after Accomplishing small steps,Small steps build great Empire.I will not say that be unique or be different,No I don't have this perception,do what is best for you,either it takes to be unique or normal,doesnt matter.But dont deviate you path away from you.The company you choose will Possibly decide where you are going,I said circumstance matters the most,but it will not be felt,because its always in your subconscious mind and don't be stagnant to where you feel Nothing constructive so don't give up your dreams for the sake of Unwanted Friendship,No you are not so Cheap,Learn To say No to the Miserable and Negative Impacts...!!

Choose the Best People,They will find most of the Solution of your problem,Even If for a Particular time the solution can't be fine,still their Persistence and Existence Will Create A Positive Vibes On You.Its up to you,no one will choose for You,No one will live for you.Life is not as much tough as you made it,Wake up everyday with a new purpose and Schedule,but never make yourself lazy,Laziness will pull you back from the competitive world,this world is very fast and accelerated,be in a competitive world,don't run away from Predicament and worries.Make It possible by Finding The Best..!!

THREE

INTROVERT AND EXTROVERT

A moment will come in unexpected expedition that you will be separated into Introvert and Extrovert intentionally or unintentionally.But virtually person choose to decide what will accommodate them.If it is an interest to be an introvert or extrovert then that is distinctive and their Inherent quality,I will not give descriptive on that,but often a person doesn't born as an introvert,situation and condition will make him that.You can't be stagnant and constant throughout this whole decade,no it is not possible,the biggest lesson you will grasp and understand in this decade only,the expedition from 15 to 25 is a life changing moment,don't make it worse by wasting time to People who don't have any great aspiration,you have the most number of hormone at this age only,You will feel the highest energetic at this age only,so don't even waste a single day,the expedition from 15 to 25 is very Perilous..!!

He is not the same person as he used to be before,time and society changed him,his perception towards freaky society had changed now,I am not blaming the whole community for the Calamity,but if a person had been deceived or betrayed then their perception will change for the whole society,yet he knows not everyone is unreliable,but he is afraid of trusting anyone,No he was not like that,he was a happy,blissful and euphoric person who always used to love his life,but something made him introvert,people deceives him,he will not trust to anyone now,he started untrusting whose who are not worth of him,he never thought that he will confront these situation in his life ,something worst and deteriorated happen with him.!!

Maybe he lose someone which he used to love more then themselves,Perhaps he had lost something interesting in himself that was so precious and intriguing,which was his boast or Proud,maybe his destiny and fate was always with him,but now it is totally opposite,maybe he used to look more attractive and alluring,but now he is no more attractive,he is a pudgy or his body structure might have change drastically,but a person doesn't look attractive by their body structure only,a real attraction is in your perception,kindness and decency.I am not talking anything hypothetical or state of delusion,these all are the reality which a youth virtually suffer,maybe a person who is reading this have these one of experience or perhaps all.A reason may be infinite but something unwanted and miserable happen to him..!!

No one who born as an extrovert will choose the introvert life until and unless they have a tragic specific reason.Everyone wants to be social,wants to enjoy like a sybarite or wants to live a life according to his desire,wants to do all the stuffs to fulfill his happiness,every person in this life has a purpose and the only difference is some have meaningful purpose and some have meaningless purpose,but a person who has a desire of something to achieve or do,their inner craving will say that at least do it once regardless of the consequences.No one wants that nobody should talk him,no one should give importance and priority to him,no one wants to live in that way,if it is one of a kind,maybe he is neurotic or lunatic and perhaps need a psychiatrist.I am not demeaning an Introvert.Its totally upon a how a person accommodate what they really want.But changing from extrovert to introvert gradually is something deplorable and imbroglio..!!

It is not easy to share your feelings to everyone,it is not possible,and you don't want to share all your problems and crisis to whole freaking society,see how you react,perceive or made a perception towards an individual or society,the same way they will treat you and give precedence and hierarchy,so don't allow everyone to know your everything,make yourself secret and crypto,the more you will make yourself secret,the more you will be mysterious.A person know you only what you allow them to know,but you have a lot of feeling,thoughts inside your brain and heart,but you don't want to propogate.Don't make your thoughts or perception perfect,no actually it is not possible,nothing can be perfect,instead make your thoughts,perception stronger and expand it in a positive way.your Inner heart and brain will decide and tell how to react and take actions on your thoughts,so make your thought more powerful..!!

There is nothing bad or conviction to be an introvert,an introvert will only know how peaceful and pacific they are after choosing to be this and separating them from the fake society.Being an Ambivert is quite Intriguing but their is nothing bad to choose a specific,the one you accommodate.Don't blame an introvert that why he chose that,no you can't ever comprehend that what may he had gone through.Judging anyone on the basis of their short confabulation is totally wrong,if you really want to know someone who you think in very rude or cruel in a funny way,talk to them in a courteous and polite way,try to give comfort to them,keep spreading love and happiness to them,after fully trusting you,they will try to be close with you.Not everyone is same and no one has the same story in life,everyone suffers from different conditions..!!

But try to be close and courteous to the introvert,they need a reliable person in life,they want love again,not always the partners love,the love which gives you happiness,if they are introvert and still they are giving you essence and importance,means they trust you and you are lucky that despite been suffered from the reliability issues someone is trusting you to let you know about themselves,don't break them again.Maybe you can be next culprit to suffer from this,the Introvert issue is the pivotal part of the expedition from 15 to 25.If you haven't suffer then its ok,maybe you are lucky,but don't scoof or be sarcastic with the one who is suffering.Don't despair them,Be with them.Been a social people and extrovert with full of energetic and happiness and coming to that point of life where you enjoy to be alone and in seclusion state is something to be considered as Poor Devil..!!

Widely persons loves to be alone from their inherent,I am not talking about this issue,they are exceptional case so don't confuse from my words,the one whose interest is to be an introvert or the one whose interest to be an extrovert is totally their innate choice,no one will go against their own happiness,so please don't be a silly to think if someone loves to be an introvert,and why even you have arise a question on this,No, I am not considering that part of been an introvert,everything has two parts,even a person has a two faces,so it doesn't mean i am demeaning introvert or giving superiority to the extrovert,but facts can't go anywhere.The expedition from 15 to 25 comes in an unexpected way and unpredictable way..!!

Learn to respect critical and predicament situations of someone,you never know that today you are making fun of anyone will cost very expensive to you,if you can't console or try to be good to someone,don't conceive or wonder that you will be happiest person all time,maybe for a specific time you will make advantage by doing atrocities or not being fair and honest,but one day you will confront yourself in the same way how you have treated them.Times changes man,everything changes in particular period of time,don't scoff or jibe to their present,learn to console and be kind hearted.Time is the only Non living object which will continuously accelerate up and down in human life and keeps reminding everyone that yes I am the most comfortable and perilous non living object.Time is the Agathokakological non living object..!!

Everyone has a personal and arbitrary choice to be an introvert,believe me an introvert will teach you virtual reality of the life,being alone will make you more conscious and your perception towards society will be more easier,An alone person will smile more but they will understand each and every aspects of the life in a better way than others.Dont scoff or ridicule anyone,it doesn't mean that you will suffer between 15 to 25 only,its totally apocryphal and delusion but most of them suffers in this expedition only,you are not aware what they had gone through,You can't even conceive that they have suffered,so respect the condition regardless of distinguishing into gender,caste or status.Either you are introvert,Extrovert or Ambivert,it's totally your choice and your happiness,Be with your Happiness..!!

FOUR

GOLDEN ERA OF SCHOOLS

From all these issues,we once have a time and maybe still we are in that stage,A stage where you starts learning your first step of your life,a stage where everyone is keen to go ,a stage where we are proud of ourselves to go,we always thought that going to this place will make our life more interesting and happier.After home,The person learnt and their upbringing has been done to this majestic place.Yes I am talking about the most Entertaining and most Humorously Hazardous place "School".We feel a positive and intriguing sense of humor whenever anyone talks about school.Each and Every Stuff which we do in school is always memorable and our emotions will be always attached to our school..!!

Merely those persons can only feel the importance and Emotions of school who is now no more in school,they only knows that this life is totally different from our school,we never thought that this life will be so tough and challenging after passing out from school.If someone is still in school,believe me you are the luckiest one,you never know that once you will come out from the school,where your life would take you.The place of 5,6,8 or maybe 10 years in the school,is still like we had enjoyed our life till the extreme extinct.A place where we had thousands of memories and full of emotions.We often feel nostalgic whenever we think of our school and the memories that is embedded in our mind for this lovable Place..!!

There is a Extreme Possibility that no one misses their school just because they love to study there.Haha yes study was the part of school,but we never consider study priority part of the school,maybe some toppers will get angry after reading this line,but this is true for most of them.Once our great scientist APJ Abdul kalam said,Marks will not make you laugh,but memories will do.Its a illusion that we go to school for the studying purpose only,no if we go to school for studying only,there will be not so much memories and emotions instill with us.Life has many variations and full of mysterious world but a person first mysterious world is their school.This was most interesting and happiest expedition from age 15 to 25 for us ..!!

There was a time when we used to bunk the classes when the most monochrome or boring period was held,without taking the permission and going to washroom hidely and then coming to class via going through the whole corridor,often seeking into the classes of another section where your best friends are,Finding the teacher which you have crush on,and if you find them and talked with them,you feel happier from inside and used to tell your friends about that.Sometimes our friends use to have fight with someone and then we all showing unity and willing to take revenge and retaliation from the opponent,just because we love of our friends so much,Maybe today we are not in touch with the school mates,but we always remember our besties of school..!!

Before a moment of appearing in exam,consoling the partner who just sit beside or perhaps behind you,the eager and enthusiasm for giving exam paper and having the fear of not studying too much and that fear was most terrified,still sometimes we can feel the fear of school exam.Maybe sometimes one of the school members succumb,and the school announces holiday,despite of lamenting and mourning we used to be happy just because we got one another day for holiday.Always waiting eagerly for the saturday to come so that we should get holidays.The best day at school time is always "Sunday".And the worst day was "Monday".No one will deny this..!!

The most exasperating and annoying moments was to wake up early in the morning and finding ties and socks if it is not in suitable place,we never wake up at first time neither we want to,some has the talent to wake up by their own but i never wake up by myself,it was the toughest thing at school time.The wind and air blowing in the morning makes us so soothing.When there was a PT day we always wait for the PT classes from the first period and wearing PT dress always makes us feel a true sportsman.Everyones feels very good after wearing that dress,maybe some have blue,red,yellow or green.Mine was red and for that reason only my favorite color is red.Some of the sports like koko,Race and 10 most common exercise we always use to play..!!

Not everyone was the same in the school,some were good in studies,somewhere good in Sports,Some in Cajoling and some were good in fighting and a type of bellicose. Thats was the beauty of the school and childhood.There were no caste,religion,status discrimation and we never used to judge the people on these stereotype things .A fear of parents teaching meeting was the most terrified fear in school.What teacher will say and how parents will react by seeing the marks,these all were literally Amazing.We all were afraid going for PTM with our parents and if we know from earlier that our marks was not good,we only know the fear that beats inside us.Sometimes we used to meet friends at PTM,so we get some relieve after seeing their faces who is too fail..!!

Sleeping in the Most boring period,perhaps its math or history but intentionally we wanted to sleep,some have the habits to eat lunch in the intervene of classes and insist everyone to eat so that he shouldn't be caught alone,some used to make weird and whirring sound,just to make the classmates laugh and take the teacher intention away from teaching.Supporting the friends in every difficult situation and always standing with them used to makes us happier.If your lover was in your section,then you think as you are the luckiest,you never miss the classes,we maybe fail in the exams but your attendance will always be 100%.I know some are feeling the same as i am telling just now.But unfortunately these all things will never come back..!!

We always used to have one favorite teacher in the class whom we always admire and gives respect to them lot,the only reason to respect them because if we do some mistakes,or breaks the school law they always used to save and intercede us.Some students always used to a fake pampering and masquerading to some teachers,in every class,at least there is one student who used to pamper a teacher just for the sake of his own benefit.And we used to hate that student in a funny way.There is at least one student who was the biggest entertainer in the class,always used to mock and ridicule the teachers,we all enjoyed those moments.These moments will never come back..!!

But gradually the times comes when we all have to leave this beautiful memories and emotion left with us.Some memories were left in school and some memories we take us with in our heart.I still remember the second last day of my school,when i have questioned myself.Where will i get all these again in life?Man you know i didn't get the answer still.We don't know but Anywhere we will be in life further,we will always remember the memories and all the naughty behaviors of our school.Don't waste your life,enjoy as much as you can,time will never come back.Maybe you can be the richest person tomorrow,but you can't buy the past again.Yes we still miss the memories of our school very much..!!

FIVE

PATIENCE

No one knows what a person is going through,so don't be rude to the peoples,give them the happiness,maybe just because of your happiness someone will start healing from inside.They say that money can buy a happiness.If money can buy happiness,Sushant singh rajput will never commit a suicide,his death was a reminde that having lavishing life and money has no connection with the inner peace,money is just importent part of life,but only inner peace can give you the happiness.Nothing is more precious then a person loves and gratitude towards the needy person.Make each and every part of your life valuable and wake everyday with a very purpose,always keeps a big desire in life,a person without desire and aspiration will never have a right path in thier life..!!

No matter,what's your status is,or any particular position you are at,what's your surrounding,how the people will treat,how they will give priority to you,whether they will concern you always or not,they remember you or not,you will be always judge on the basis of worth you are.You will never be satisfied with less worth of yours.A person can make themselves peace and happy only when they will have a satisfaction of something.Satisfaction is variable,it will be never constant.But giving love and healing someone's pain is bigger than satisfaction of ours.Satisfaction will make you happy only for a particular period of time,but doing best and spreading love not for yourself but for the loved ones will make you also happy,and the person who loves you will always be proud of you..!!

We always wants what we see with our eyes,we will be never comfortable with what we have,but that's ok it is good not to choose comfort zone,being in comfort zone is the most irritating and perilous,i will never choose to be in comfort zone,it is trend amongst the mediocre people that we will do some good work in life and comes in a comfort zone.No,I am not born to live in comfort zone,I want what i always dream of and whatever it takes to do i am ready for that.But it will not come to you easily,the perspiration and perseverance will take you there in the life and the enthusiasm for your desire will take you to the peak.We all are very young now,we all are energetic and exuberant,don't give shit to the bullshits,they will always demean you.The only way you can rise is have confidence and faith in yourself..!!

You are the starring of your own vehicles,all the vehicles outside you is your circumstance,if you will not drive properly you may have accident and you may die from that,but no one is responsible for your death,your own irresponsibility will kill you.No one has accountability for your death,so its your duty to drive you starring in proper way,in the same way your life is,we all are full of anxiety,problems,jealousy,family issue,financial problems,love failure at the age of 15 to 25,but you don't have to faint,its ok to fall down but rise up as much time as you can.A person will never reach the peak so easily,no one has reached his/her with that easily,without suffer and determination you even can't live in your society,how can you become great.Great Peoples is great at their works..!!

Your Positive Thinking and Intellectual Mindset is equivalent to the Extreme success chances and Your negativity and Stereotype mindset is equivalent to Extreme Failure chances.!!But don't rely on non livings things,Money is an important part of your life,but it is not the key to happiness.Be always kind to the people,the person will give you blessings,these all are the true happiness.I am about to end my book soon.I know you don't share your problems to everyone,i know how you are feeling right know,i know what loves failure goes through,i know the importance of loosing something,i am like you man, but please its a request don't lose hope but at the same time don't move far from hardwork and determination..!!

How your past gone,how you suffered,how you feel,these all things doesn't matter until and unless you come out as a warrior and shine.No one will listen your thoughts and struggle if you will not achieve the height.Don't share or explain your problems with the wrong people,they will only enjoy the moments,a bad person will never understand your suffer and never admire your talent,so don't waste time in sharing or proving to the wrong person.Always work in silence,one day everyone will see your success,just be patience because no one will give the example of you until you reach your goal.Patience is the biggest weapon of you.Utilize it in proper way,Many have a talent to achieve something,but just because they can't bear patience they give up or relinquish their dreams..!!

Patience is the biggest gift you can have.Inbuilt this habit in yourself,nothing can come to you at quick time,you have to be patience enough to endure and work for it.Loosig hope and patience will only lead to destruction.So keep patience and don't undermine if something not comes in your way.Wait everything will be fine at the right time.Be tough,don't reveal everything to everyone,keeps secrets,keep promising yourself,keep working hard in silent,don't show off.Those who show off is the biggest stupid in the world.If you are worth of it,people will acknowledge you one day.Be smart with yourslef and others.I am about to end my book soon now,so this way my opinion and interpretation and maybe i had told some of my words here which i never reveal ever to anyone..!!

Patience is everything,yaa it's everything,a moment will come in your life when you will lose everything,nothing will go in your way,very less people will love you,you will lose loving yourself,people will start objecting you and criticizing you,you will feel inferior from inside,everything will be gone,only your creativity and patience will be your best friend at that time.Maybe some have these moments going on now in life,a person can't heal everything instantly and can't expect that everything will be cured promptly.Your patience and your Hope will take you out from the bad times and Quagmire.So don't take your life so easy,don't lose hope that nothing will come back,no i said time is the best non living object,it will change,just be positive and be around with positive peoples..!!

Your life is not too small,a person who had a extreme suffer and bad times and comes out as a shining example will teach you the biggest lessons of your life.Almost,we all are at that positions,many have lost many things in their life in this small expedition of our life,the expedition from 15 to 25 is very critical for all of us.You are not a loser,please don't depressed,don't suppress your thoughts and talent,make out in a different way,I know how it feels,i am too suffering from Failures,i know how it feels to you or how your heart aches and your heart is paining from so long time but still you are not giving up.You are great man,just don't quit.A time will come soon,you will be there where you want yourself,"Please Just don't quit"..!!

If a person smile,it doesn't mean he is happier,maybe he is hiding the biggest pain behind him smile,don't judge in that way,you never know what he is going through.The person who hides the pain and shows fake smile is called eccedentesiast.I love you all but keep working hard for yourself and I pray that you reach the highest peak in your life.Maybe I am not a Author or don't want to brag myself but these all are the thoughts which I always wanted to share with you all.Maybe or almost many of them is suffering from the same things,only the person who suffers will know the pain of that suffering."I know how it feels from the inside but Man Time always comes with a new life and one day everything will change"

SIX

MENTAL HEALTH IS UNDERRATED

We all are going through some problems in our life.Some have the anger issue in life and some are having laziness issues in life but all these are in visible form.People can see your anger,tensed,sadness,injured and your outer behavior. I am angry with my parents because they don't buy the stuffs for me what i told them, parents can see your anger.I am tired because of my full hectic college schedule,people can see my tiredness.I am tensed become i am not convinced with what i wanted,everyone around me can see me tensed.I had a minor accident last night with bike and i get some injuries,but doctors healed my wounds by giving medicines.I am having a relationship with someone and had a conflict in corridor,my friends noticed it and try to manage the conflicts with my partner.I am smiling because of funny comedian is entertaining me,everyone sees my laughing and made a perception that i am happy with my smile.

But wait, all these are your physical attitude and behavior through which people make perception about your existence aur who you are.But wait,what about mental health? What is mental health? People ever consider your mental health? The truth and harsh reality is no.People don't even know what you are going through.There is a difference between your physical health and mental health.I am not talking about the medical mental health.This mental health is about your soul,about your behavior,about your sadness,about your happiness and painfulness inside you which people will never see in you.This mental health is underrated in every aspects because the reality is it can't be seen to people.

You show your anger to people,people will consider it but what about angriness inside you which is stopping you to express to people,because you know this anger is something which people can't solve it.And ultimately you quench your angriness inside you only.People will see you your laziness but do they know from where this laziness is coming and why? Maybe you don't like that work that's why you are lazy,maybe you don't want to do it now,but what if you love to do some work and that need intense hard work,you will quickly get up and do that work which you are interested in.Its not about laziness,it's about the priority that you give.But people will never understand your perception of laziness..! I am angry with my parents that they dont buy for me what I told them.They will consider my anger and convince me.But we only know how badly i wanted that stuff from my parents but ok i will satisfy my mental wish.

I am tired because of my college 's hectic schedule. They will just see my tiredness and give me one mango juice to get back my energy.But no one will ask why I am so tired? What are the things that I have done today that make me feel tired? Does that tiredness even benefit me? How much i worked hard today so i am feeling so dull.No one will ask all these and ultimately you will convince your tiredness inside you and take a long nap.I had a minor accident,and and got injured,every1 will start giving sympathy and affection.But can they feel my inner pain? Can they feel my painful places which i got injured and that doesnt let me sleep whole night.No they cant feel,you can only feel your wounds.I had a conflict in my relationship and my friends made a superficial solution for this relation and thought that we are happy again in relation.No one knows how is this relation,the irritation,the pain,the broken heart and disturbed mind,can they feel all these things?Can they feel my mental disturbance which i am going through from this relation?No they can just give sympathy.

I am smiling because of some comedy shows and simultaneously people noticed my smile and made a perspective that i am genuinely happier from my soul.Can they even think that this smile was just to forgot for sometimes all the heartbroken and hurtful story of my life.Can they think that this smile is not genuine,even i don't know last time when did i smile from bottom of my heart.Everyone has a burning desire to become something in life,which they are daily doing work for their desire,can anyone even guess,how much hard work is required to come close to that burning desire.No no and no,people will only judge you by your behavior and physical attitude.You know your pain,you know your struggling phase and you know how to fight it back,you mind is that engine which will take all your body parts with you.So you have to prepare even tougher to your engine.!!

This is our outer ability and inner disability that if we want to share our mental problems to someone we can't share.So what's the ultimate solution of this mental problem? How are you gonna tackle this mental problem with yourself? Till when you will suffer from your mental irritation.The reality is you can't share all your indignation and angriness to everyone.I will not give you the advice that do this and do that for your mental problems.Me and you are connected with these lines.So its better to make a combined perception and do at least something for this mental problems.Everyone has their own situations which is totally different in context so we can't give clarification at all aspects of this problem.

The first problem with the peoples are they don't know actually where you stand and what are your strength and that's why there is a negativity injected in you by yourself that eventually makes your strength also even weaker.you lose your confidence,you lose your worth just because of the people perception made for you on the just basis of your outer perpection.You will feel guilty,you will ask god,why this is happening with me?Why is my worth not shown to people? Why can't people see my strength?I can do more than what people think of me.You can say that you alone can go high but in reality you need support,you need someone to support you,at least from your loved ones. Surrounding folks are subconsciously connected to you.

So what's the ultimate solution of this underrated mentality.See you cant die like this within yourself or maybe i will not say that by doing this your mental problems will be 100% solved and you will be happier always from inside,no all these are bullshit,keeping your happiness and sadness is a part of life,you can't sustain always with either of these.Maybe first see what actually your mental problems are disturbing you,then try to find out the people around you who actually understands you,discuss your problems,say the pros and cons of the situation,take it out from your heart and brain,at least it will feel lighter,maybe they will understand and try to give you genuine sympathy and possible solutions of that mental pain.It will relieve you,remember words have more power then your non existing imagination.You can come out from this mental disability,all you need is to share everything to the loved ones.

Now,you can't share everything to your parents or friends or maybe anyone in your life.So choose the people wisely according to your perception who can actually try to heal your mental problems. Don't keep it inside,it will kill you day by day but at the same time,don't tell everyone also.Its universal truth that not everyone will actually understand who you are,what is your worth? What can you do better? What do you actually need from life? People are only interested in the their interest,Until they are satisfied with you,they are above you,they will be happy with you,people will always try to make their justification superior because only thing they need is that they are more superior than you.The day you work hard,do good stuffs,cross the comfort zone,the same people will start pulling you down.Thats how the psychology works,that's how the mindset works,and that is reality

Share with your true friends,tell them the problems,believe me true friends are more then a soulmate,its the one-fourth of your reason of improvement if you genuinely have one.And in the same way,try to see your loved ones also,if thier face show sadness,ask them whats the reason,observe it,talk to them,try to heal thier problems,understand the psychology of your loved ones,they also need you,Bro you are not just born for yourself,you are for the peoples who needs you,who needs your support,dont let anyone die from mental health.Dont let anyone do suicide ,just because thier was no one to listen them,so they did a suicide by taking thier mental problems with them.Unity is strength,support the power,support the process,support the hardwork,heartbroken peoples needs sympathy and support more then money and fame.Promise me,you will heal the mental health of someone who needs you..!!

SEVEN

IMAGINATION AND IMPLEMENTATION

Well we all know that once we were child and we grown up in some extent.One great leader said that tell me whom you are surrounded with and i will tell you who you will be in the future.We all are confined to our surrounding thoughts and made a mindset like that.For example you can't learn chinese language in india without working on it specifically.But in the same time,if the same guy will be surrounded by chinese language,he will start learning As soon as possible,so the conclusion is it's not about how intense you are or how good you are at your faith,its always matter subconsciously that how you are bounded by your surroundings.

For example,if you are surrounded by peoples who have low-esteem ,narrow minded and you have a high esteem and having a broad minded,despite of self belief and confidence,somewhere these surroundings will pull you back.They will indirectly start making you to question about yourself,you will start doubting yourself.And in vice versa if you don't have such high esteem and have a little narrow mindset and if you are surrounded by intellectual peoples,despite of having narrow minded,this surrounding will help you indirectly,you will gain positivity from these surrounding subconsciously,you will become more confidence,that will push you from low grade to at least think something constructive in life.This is how surrounding impact in your life.

And all these come from your Imagination.Remember,imagination is more powerful than knowledge.Imagination is like a water,if you throw a glass of water,it become shapeless,it can flow anywhere.In the same way Imagination is limitless,imagination is infinite,you can flow in any direction.But that's how it differs a normal person from a successful person.Every human being imagine,but how your imagination works,that is considerable,at what extent your imagination can go,and in which perspective it can imagine,all these matters.Every human being is born with same mind but how after a years same mind is changed to different mindset.It's imagination which separates from mind to mindset.

Your first step to success is your imagination.A guy who is surrounded by intellectuals and having a lavish background but still not having a greater imagination will never succeed at the level of mindset.But the other guy who is from a small background but his ambition and level of thinking is high,then that is only the first step of success.People lack in this only,they want to achieve something but they never imagine how to achieve that ambition.Imagination is that part of mind which create your vision.Hardworking,following the right path and perseverance are secondary source.All these can be only done when you can imagine to do something constructive.

Don't watch unnecessary entertainment Tv shows,these shows will only take your mind to comfort zone.Remember one thing,the advertisement or shows or movies whatever it is,if it doesnt let you think about it,it is producing negative garbage in your mind.The pleasure and enjoyment in the shows and movies will never make your mind innovative and productive.I am not against TV or any shows,until and unless you are watching just for the purpose of enjoyment for sometimes it is good for you,but don't make it a habit,it will be harmful.Make your mindset powerful.Read books,read novels,read magazines,read authentic newspaper,watch creative movies.All these things will make your psychological part more strong.The more psychologically powerful you will be,the more you will think creative and constructive in life.

Reading will make you more innovative,as like you are reading this book now,it is going in your brain cells and making you to imagine how vs why.Talk to people who are working hard for their life.They will give you some hints for life purpose.That conversation between you and that person will make you to imagine that productive conversation in a more better way. Watch movies which has moral,remember your thought process is a reflection of your movies.What you watch,what you read is what you will think.Dont gossip,dont be involved in unnecessary stuffs,all these will only make your mind garbage.A fish living in small pond will only imagine that this is the whole world.Fish will never imagine that there is oceans and oceans outside this world,because that fish never came out from his pond.Don't be that fish,be a whale who flow and swim through the whole ocean..

Play games,but just for the sake of enjoyment for brain,not for the pleasure of soul.Even i was addicted to games,still i play games,but now i know the value of time and i know how to utilize games for the purpose of enjoyment only.Dont watch rubbish movies which does not have any morals,all these will put garbage only.All the tv shows which shows fiction romantic love stories are just bullshits.After that only,you make a perception that i want one partner,i need it desperately by just non existing tv shows.First become a worthy man,girls are not going anywhere.Eventually girls will also choose a worthy and successful man at the end.This is indeed reality,and vice versa for the girls also.Successful person will always have a big library then big TV,so invest more times in library not at TV shows.Your existence matter,don't spoil it,your respect matters,don't give it in someones hand.Imagine as big that one day someone imagine your imagination.

Watch some podcasts which is based on biography on some successful person.Listen the speeches of legend who will tell you that how they struggle for this life and what are the problems they face to overcome these hurdle.Watch the entrepreneur interview,they will tell you how to be creative at business marketing.You don't have following people surrounded by all these ability but you have your social media and mobile,use it in a proper way.Read the biography of the legends,read the psychology of human mindset,read the human history and evolution of humans and earth,this will let you know about past that will give you vision about the future.Legends doesnt born legends,they work on them then they become.Imagination doesn't come until you imagine to learn something productive.

If it cost nothing to imagine,why can't we imagine as big as possible.Why people start criticizing each other,why people start trolling others,why dispute begins between two authority,why two people debate with each other,it's just because they both have different imagination.Your imagination makes difference with others.But imagination doesn't go in a irrelevant way.It should be under relevant perspective.Simply for example,you imagine that you want to pluck the moon and give to your partner,which we sees in the movies,this is not possible so i am not talking about hypothetical imagination.It should be authentic which is under your circumstance but it should be unique and beyond your present mindset.

It should never be stagnant,imagination doesn't have any finite point.It should always be for the positiveness of people and yourself,you just have to imagine because there is no definition of right and wrong for imagination.Imagination is just creative,imagination is limitless,imagination can make you travel everywhere but at the same time solely imagination should not be the only vision but how to implement in a positive and focused way is how your imaginative power will works.So start your every task and goal of life with creative imagination and constructive implementation.Imagination has nothing connection with hard work and perseverance.You just need a healthy mindset to imagine the best for your success.

EIGHT

YOUR EXISTENCE MATTERS

Well,we all have been curious about the fantasy and behavior of the peoples.We all are busy searching what others are obsessed with and always try to find flaws in others.For example if someone who has some money and fame and is connected to you.We intentionally praise and try to make space with the peoples like that irrespective of your self respect and reputation.Everyone deserves respect and is universal behavior but have you asked yourself that your respect matters the most because it is only you who will know the value of your self respect.We never thought about ourselves.We are busy in knocking someone else door always.Lavishing and high standard people is more reputed than your own reputation.This is the illusion we are giving birth in our mind.

If you approach any celebrity,you will do whatever makes them happy just to convince them that you are biggest admirer of them.You will follow them,sometimes you will have a dispute with other peoples for that celebrity irrespective of self worth.Why if someone superior does wrong and you make a perception that he is superior than maybe there is something right in that what he has done.But in the same way if you do any mistake,you curse yourself,you see yourself as hopeless person,you see yourself as a worthless person.Why can't you thought to be a celebrity?Why can't you can upgrade yourself in your life? Everything is in your hand.Just your perception made a difference with other people.

Why do we give so much respect to people who don't even know you? Why do we admire people whom you don't even meet once?Why do we fight for the celebrities who never discuss our problems? Why do we argue for the people who don't know our priority? Have you questioned yourself? Who am I? Why do I always connect my inner soul with someone's outer looks? Have you ever questioned what are the shortcomings i have from that celebrity which made him star today?Why can't i like hime?No you never questioned yourself because you were busy admiring and praising someone who doesn't even exist in front of you ever? Why people suicide for someone?Why are people making human beings into gods? All these questions will always be non existing in your mind until and unless you will start questioning yourself.

Have you ever asked yourself that your self-existence matters or not.Why you lose your reputation for someone.Praising and admiring is not a problem but why you are connecting yourself internally with someones outer appearance just because of their looks and habits.Why you start giving more respect to someone who is not worth of it but just because you will have an advantage with them so you are more conscious about that person.Remember,expectation will always lead to sadness.You expect from someone who has no connection with your problems,who have no connections with your priority,who has no connection with your parents priority.then why are we giving our expectations to the people who is just little rich and more civilized than you?

Your self existence matter,you are born alone.Your self respect will always be with you.Keep it always high,you are not born to do some shoddy works,you are not born to work under someone,you are not born to do hard works only,you are not born to convince anyone,you are not born to suppress your irritation for someone.You are not born to cry for someone.You are born for yourself,you are born for your happiness,you are born for your priority,you are born to make proud to your parents,you are born to make proud to yourself.Your existence on earth matters.

No celebrity will come and heal your wounds when you will be totally broken.No political leader will come and wipe your tears when you will be alone.Alone doesnt means weak.Alone means powerful,you need guts to fight alone for yourself.No money and fame folks will come and heal your soul from the money.You have your respect,your existence matters,just go and ask your parents that what they mean to you.You are only celebrity,politician and moneyman for them.I am not blaming anyone neither demeaning them,i am just trying to give clarity that your existence is above from all these thing.

Instead of peeking someone else life,work for yourself,it will make you more independent from everyone.Be independent,you will always take your mind and heart everywhere with yourself.Your priority should be you and your work not someone movies and entry.Make yourself worth,think in such a whey,that why i am the one who follow someone and seek for the attention.Can i do something in this world that people seek attention for me,can i do something that will make my worth more stronger.Working on yourself will always be the best option for yourself.Everyone has been given one life,don't invest in someone's else life,do something that you didn't remember people but people will always remember you.

Whenever people try to approach you,first observe what are their ultimate goals with you,what's their perspective meeting with you,and dont be servile for some little self praise and admiration.Your admiration doesn't have a certificate with someone else,your admiration is within yourself.It's not people fault,it's only you who look and stalk behind them just for the sake of some dignity and fame.You will never understand your life until and unless you will keep stalking people on the basis of society perception with that people.And believe me they will only use you for their purpose,they will satisfy you with some temporary support and money but that doesn't even actually matters for you.

They are not going to live with you whole life.Once you lose yourself,you will start losing everything within yourself,your aim,your goal and your achievements.You are not special,a ordinary guy but thats cool,its special to be ordinary and feel special for yourself.It's ok to be ordinary and make them feel special for loved one around you.No one is hopeless and worthless.It's just a human psychology which people implement in their minds.Change your mindset and see the results.This will be totally your fault if you indulge your inner soul and dignity in someone's else life.People will always choose according to their need and pleasure but you have the option to be yourself or be a slave.

Learning and admiring the people will always a good idea,but don't be a puppet for someone,it will make your self respect destroy.You are already a champion because you are amongst the bundles of sperms fighting for the lives and ultimately you won the race.You are already a winner from god grace.You already came to this world with courage and fighting spirit.Give value to your existence,you can't live another live after this life.Your life is special in a special way.Just remember two rule throughout this whole topic and one is remembering that your existence matters and second is that never forget the first rule.

NINE

UNCOMFORTABLE ZONE MAKES YOU STRONGER

Well we all are running for money and pleasure in life so that we could achieve something in life.Everyone is running here and there for some purpose to achieve their wish and desire.Everyone wants to be rich and in comfort zone.This life is just running for lavishing and superiority life for people.Comfort zone will always give you pleasure and happiness which most of the people choose to take.From the birth till the death,every human being is searching for comfort zone.No one will satisfy with their comfort zone.The only difference is everyone has a different level and position of being in a comfort zone.For example A wants to be comfort like B because B is more comfortable then A and B wants to be comfort like C because C Is more comfortable then B.So its all about position and hierarchy.

For example if you get a chance to eat pizza and coconut juice,then your psychological part will always choose to eat pizza because it gives more pleasure and taste for your brain and tongue but in reality that pizza is harmful for your health if you make a habit of eating.Despite of knowing this,you will always prefer to choose pizza because it gives more comfort.Other examples is if you have an option of sleeping or going for a morning walk,your dopamine(which release hormone for pleasure and hard work) will always choose to go for sleep,it will give your body relax and you will be freely lying on a bed and sleeping,but you will not choose to go for morning walk because it takes hard work and courage to wake up in the morning.

Sleeping will always gives you comfort.Why we feel sleepy while studying because dopamine will always release a hormone which will send to your brain that sleeping is more comfortable and cozy but studying need focus and concentration which you mind is not ready for,so you will choose to sleep rather then studying.In the same way even if you are feeling sleepy and suddenly you decided to play and then you will start playing and you literally enjoy it.But where is your nap gone?That's again dopamine will release a hormone which will force you to play because it gives more pleasure and you will always sacrifice something for your pleasure.All these instincts are going in a comfort zone.

We make ourselves to always be in a comfort zone.Dopamine reacts in both ways,if you are addicted to comfort zone,it will always give a signal to be in a comfort zone,for example if you give a doggy one piece chapati,he will always remember that food and will come near your house for the search of that chapati.In the same way,you have inculcated the addiction of pleasure in you mind so mind will always search for pleasure and comfort zone.And that's what your reality is connected with your zone,We have always searched for happiness,pleasure but we never consider the context of all these things.You can't get pleasure all the time,in the same way you can get pain every time.The context matters in human psychology.

But have you ever tried to satisfied with your uncomfortable zone.No because you were never used to be in uncomfort zone.Thats why consistency of anything matters the most.You cant be unique or you can't be in such a way that people will see you in different perspective if you will be normal or think like a normal.Uncomfortable zone is tough,no it is tougher,oh sorry maybe i have done a typing mistake but uncomfortable zone is the toughest ever.Being in reality and other aspect is being in fake perception makes a lot different in human appearance and ethos.You can try your 100% to show yourself superior to this society but deep inside you know your reality that where you stand.

You can't sustain in the uncomfortable zone in the beginning,it will irritate you,it will tell you to find pleasure in something else but there is one whole different aspect of uncomfortable zone.It will make you strong,no sorry it will make you stronger.Ahh i again mistyped it but surely uncomfortable zone makes you the strongest.People who overcome unnecessary emotional trapped are the ones who fought for himself and makes his mind strong in uncomfortable zone.People who overcome unnecessary mental gossiping were once fighting for himself in uncomfortable zone.You can't work hard for one day and say that i was in uncomfortable zone for one day but nothing happens.Haha it doesn't work in this way.One day perception will always be temporary pleasure but not be long term effective.

You can't be normal and you cant be great at the same time.Mind clarity and seeing world in a different perspective is the outcome of burning yourself in uncomfortable zone.Being selfish maybe a selfishness for mediocre people but for me being selfish is knowing and giving attention to your own worthy.If you can't do something good for yourself then how can you will be a happier face for someone else so selfishness is a part of your self development.So selfishness has a different perspective in different people minds.At Least be selfish for yourself.I don't mean to say that dont think good about someone or feel happy for someone,my selfish topic is being discussed for other aspects.So dont be confuse.Be selfish,but for your work and dedication.

You can't crack UPSC or NEET by going to coaching and doing some normal formality as students.Your whole focus should be on knowing how to be the best in particular exams.Sitting and exhausting your mind to grab all the stuffs needed for the exams.You have to cross the limitation of your learning and understanding ability of brain then only you can do something great in that exams.It need focus,it needs dedication with 0% excuse.The ultimate moral is it needs uncomfortable zone to be under 100 ranks out of lakhs.It needs days and month of everyday of hard work and mental toughness to reach your goal,it need mind clarity and self discipline to reach your worth.It needs courage and lots of courage to be happy in uncomfortable zone.

You can't just thought of making your physique better and it happened.It actually need guts to make a mindset of going gym and hitting your body.1 day or 1 month will not be even enough to satisfy yourself in gym.It needs lots of hard work each and every day,no the actual is each and every second of that hour

Results will not come in 1 day or 1 month,the consistency and patience in uncomfortable zone will make your body what you wanted to be.It's not easy,but nothing is impossible in front of your burning desire for any particular stuff.Uncomfortable zone in gym will take you somewhere you will be always proud of.Not everyone can grab this quality,but one who actually wants to do something in life will know the pleasure and irritation of uncomfortable zone.

So never be cool and show yourself worthy when you haven't been to uncomfortable zone ever.Its your perception that you are the best but you are just peeking in your lake.Each and every second many are going above and below you.You can be comfortable in any moment of your life.Once you reach a particular level,you will desire for something else,but that time you doesn't need to be in uncomfortable zone,you already passed out your zone,you only need some focus and attention.But now,if you find nothing special in life,make your uncomfortable zone your friend and start seeing the miracle in yourself.Uncomfortable decides your hierarchy position in life.So say again "uncomfortable zone makes you stronger".

TEN

NO ONE WILL BE ALWAYS SPECIAL

We as a human being is always eager to get attention from the people we want.Sometimes the condition is like we lost the actual self being.From the understanding zone of our life till now,we always have a subconscious perception of making special to one whom we want.We try to keep stalking the person where they are and what is going in their life.A human being is always obsessed of making someone special.Speciality means you always want to connect with the person whom you want to be special.A desire to make special someone will always be in human nature until their breath flows irrespective of the consequences.Parents love will always be the special part in someone's life.

But more than their parents,human being try to peek speciality whom he doesn't even know properly.Thats a human psychology,irrespective of race,complexion if we inbuilt in our mind to give someone priority, we will try our utmost level to make that person special.Most of the cases it happened in opposite genders.But what if we make someone special and it feels special to make someone special.But have you ever questioned yourself that how long that person should be special for you.I am not clarifying here that don't make someone special,its useless.No,not at all.That is the strongest moment when you have someone who makes you feel special.

But at what perception does the speciality work? What if someone more superior than you comes into that person's life and they get attracted towards them.It's obvious that human nature attracts more good vibes and stuffs.What if a more good-looking or rich person comes into their life and they get attracted towards themselves?Do you have any guarantee that the one who is special today for you will always be special for you? What if the person loses interest in you and someone more classy attracts them with their words and body language.What if someone who has a good dressing sense and more knowledgeable than you comes in their life and take them away from you because every aspects of human life,there's always someone who is better than you.

It's not always work that if you have a good heart then that person will always be with you.Not everyone is like that,not everyone is true,so you have to think logically to overcome all these barriers.You have any certificate that this person will always be special for me until i want.Nooo,The problem for making someone special is we lost ourselves,we lost our dignity,we lost our self being.Why cant u make special someone who will always be with you.Who is that? Obviously its you,make yourself special.You are special and you will always be special.The problem for making someone special is you that even a small disagreement will make your heart sad because you always expect that from that person to be what you want,not what she wants or what is real.

Make special,there is nothing wrong in that,but value your worth,don't give your expensive value to someone else hand in the name of speciality.That is what the negative aspect of being special.People always consider that if i am special in someone life than the person is in our control.Don't pretend or don't behave like that.Make that person special but be always yourself.There is a thick barrier between making someone special and making yourself being special.Never compromise yourself being speciality for someone else speciality.

ELEVEN

SHOWING OFF IS STUPIDITY

This is the easiest and toughest topic someone will go through.It's easy because you don't need much hard to show off.But it's tough because deep inside you know who you actually are.But the question arises is why do we need to show off? To hide our weakness? To show to the people that I am also from a rich family? To prove to people that I am also worthy of it? Does it really impact logically on your life? Have you ever questioned yourself why you show off.We always think what people will think before thinking what actually matters to me.

Logically you will get negative impact on your life if you will not portray actual that who you are.Because you are the one who knows yourself very well.You can impress people by showing off but what will you tell yourself when you will be alone.You can't lie same stuffs always to the people.There will be one moment that people will also understands your reality.Do you ever thought that when you are showing off and when you are alone then that your mind tells you you.Doesn't it feels irritated to portray yourself fake to the people.Doesn't it feels awkward to lie to yourself

Showing off just boost your imaginary perception of self being.You cant always show off to people who doesn't give shit to your stuffs.Quality can be seen without displaying anything from your mouth and body language.Showing off kills your passion.It doesn't allow you to work hard for your goal,because you have inbuilt in your mind,that by just showing off,people are impressed with you so you don't have to work much hard.Because ultimately you want that people should consider you as worthy or be impressed by your superiority,and showing off is the easiest method.

But it can't be permanent,you will fall down very soon.Don't do it,be realistic,even if you have 1 percent quality,portray your 1 percent quality but don't show off.If you want to be extraordinary you can't show off,work harder and then achieve your goals and then show as much as you can.But don't do that before,Question to yourself? You are not clever by doing this,you are actually stupid,It is loosening your self identity.By showing off,your mind will never let you to work for your passion,the brain will not allow because you have maked a mindset to just show off and gain superiority.

Start from the zero,take time but try to erase this mindset of showing off,you think you are smarter,you are superior but realistically nothing positive impact will happen for you.It kills every positive and constructive ideas and vision.Think then you are alone,that what actually impacts by showing off.If you are genuine to yourself,you will get the answer.Showing off is stupidity.It will cost nothing to say something which actually even does not exist,so work on this if you are victim of this topic.

9 798886 297553

Printed by Libri Plureos GmbH in Hamburg,
Germany